DEATH IS NOTHING AT ALL

Canon Henry Scott Holland

Designed and illustrated by Paul Saunders

SOUVENIR PRESS

Death is nothing at all . . .
I have only slipped away into
the next room . . .

I AM I and you are you . . .

whatever we were to each other
that we are still.

CALL me by my old familiar name, speak to me in the easy way which you always used.

PUT no difference into your tone; wear no forced air of solemnity or sorrow.

LAUGH as we always laughed at
the little jokes we enjoyed
together.

PLAY, smile, think of me, pray
for me.

LET my name be ever the household word that it always was.

LET it be spoken without effect,
without the ghost of a shadow
on it.

LIFE means all that it ever meant.

IT IS the same as it ever was; there
is absolutely unbroken
continuity.

WHAT is this death but a negligible accident?

WHY should I be out of mind
because I am out of sight?

I AM just waiting for you, for an interval, somewhere very near, just around the corner . . .

A<small>LL</small> is well.

In affectionate memory of
Ralph Vernon-Hunt
23rd MAY 1923 – 10th NOVEMBER 1987

This Edition first published 1987 by Souvenir Press Ltd,
43 Great Russell Street, London WC1B 3PA
and simultaneously in Canada

Reprinted 1990, 1991, 1992, 1994, 1995

ISBN 0 285 62824 0

Printed in Great Britain by
Redwood Books,
Trowbridge, Wiltshire